WORK IT, GIRL

BEYONCÉ KNOWLES

WORK IT, GIRL

RULE THE MUSIC SCENE LIKE QUEEN BEYONCÉ KNOWLES

Written by
Caroline Moss

Illustrated by
Sinem Erkas

Chapter 1

You're Going To Be A Star

Beyoncé Gisele Knowles was shy. That was the best word for it. Shy. During recess at school, when all of her classmates would pair off or play games in groups, Beyoncé usually kept to herself. While the children talked and played, Beyoncé watched them, wondering what it might be like to be able to not be so self-conscious about, well, everything! She was always worrying what people were going to think of her, and it made her anxious. She just liked to stay quiet and observe the world around her.

BEING THE CENTER OF ATTENTION DID NOT INTEREST BEYONCÉ.

Beyoncé's mom and dad, Tina and Mathew, noticed this. They thought it was okay for their daughter to be shy—because of course it is!—but they were worried that she was missing out on some fun experiences because of her fear of putting herself out there. When Beyoncé was seven years old, Tina had a brilliant idea.

"Beyoncé," her mom said to her one day after school with a big smile. "I was thinking about signing you up for a dance class. What do you think?"

"A dance class?" Beyoncé repeated. Her palms began to get a little sweaty and she could feel her heart beating really, really fast. "Hmmm…" She wiped her hands on her pants.

Even though the first feeling she felt deep in her belly was nervousness, the second feeling she felt was excitement, because she did like to dance and perform in her bedroom. Sometimes she'd pretend her hairbrush was the microphone and that her little sister, Solange, was her backup dancer or singer. Did her mom know that? Had she ever heard them singing and dancing in the bedroom? She must have. Solange was not nearly as shy as Beyoncé was. But dancing in front of other people? Just the thought of it made butterflies appear in Beyoncé's stomach. A whole family of butterflies!

"Think about it!" said Tina.

So Beyoncé thought and thought. She thought during breakfast, she thought during dinner, she thought during math class (whoops!). But still, she didn't know what to do. Yes? Or no? Try something new and possibly fail or embarrass herself? Or stay safe in her comfort zone?

SHE WENT TO BED THAT NIGHT AND DREAMED OF BEING ON STAGE. THE CROWD IN HER DREAMS CHEERED AND CLAPPED. SHE GOT A STANDING OVATION AND AUDIENCE MEMBERS TOSSED ROSES TO HER ON THE STAGE.

Beyoncé awoke from her dreams beaming from ear to ear. She put on her slippers and walked downstairs to the breakfast table. She knew what she was going to tell her mom.

"Okay, I'll try it." Beyoncé announced. "I'll try the dance class."

Her mother clapped her hands in joy. Her dad nodded his head in approval.

"That's great, Beyoncé!" Mathew gave his daughter a hug. "When do classes start, Tina?"

Tina Knowles checked her calendar, and flipped through some pages. "Let's see, let's see, dance class..." She moved her fingers across the page. "Aha! Next... Thursday! At 4:30pm. After school."

Beyoncé felt the butterflies come back again. This time she tried to tell herself that they weren't nervous butterflies, but excited ones. It helped.

Boy, was she happy with the choice she made! Soon, Beyoncé was dancing all the time. She would learn choreography in class and then go home and practice in her bedroom. She'd watch herself in the mirror in her bedroom to make sure she was getting the moves just right. Sometimes Solange would peek inside her bedroom from the hallway to watch her big sister.

"You wanna learn?" Beyoncé asked Solange. She nodded.

Soon, Beyoncé felt herself mastering the steps. Her teacher, Miss Darlette, would encourage her to move to the front of the room so that the other kids in the class could look to her if they needed help. When she performed on stage, she exuded confidence and ease. Her parents and sister looked at each other, smiling. They were so proud!

One day, Beyoncé was sitting on the floor after class. She was stretching her legs to make sure she didn't get any cramps. Soon, she was the last kid in the room. Miss Darlette was at the tape player, when she noticed Beyoncé and walked over to her, crouching down so that they were making direct eye contact.

"Beyoncé, I want to tell you something," Miss Darlette said. "You are gonna be so big, the whole world is gonna know you."

"I am?" Beyoncé looked at her with a smile.

"Yes. You are."

Chapter 2

A Girl Group Named Girls Tyme

• • • • • • • • • • • •

In no time, Beyoncé's shyness was a thing of the past and she could not get enough of the spotlight on stage. Her parents were so excited. They loved to see Beyoncé blossom! Soon, Beyoncé and Solange were making up their own choreography in their bedrooms and singing as they danced. They didn't even mind when their parents would peek in the room to catch them performing. That might have embarrassed Beyoncé before but not anymore.

When Beyoncé was nine years old, she still hadn't shaken her love for dance and singing, but she was looking for a new challenge. Her dad had a great idea.

"There are auditions for a girl group in downtown Houston next week," he told Beyoncé on their way home from dance class one day. "I think you should go for it."

THIS TIME BEYONCÉ DIDN'T NEED TO THINK ABOUT WHAT HER ANSWER WOULD BE. "I'M IN!" SHE EXCLAIMED.

The auditions were a little nerve-racking, because there were just so many girls there. All of them had talent and all of them wanted to be in the girl group. Beyoncé felt those butterflies appear again. Were they nerves or excitement? She decided they could be both.

When Beyoncé approached the judges she looked them right in the eye and smiled, like her dad had reminded her to do.

"Hi, I'm Beyoncé!" she said. Then she began her audition. She moved and grooved, nailed all of her steps, and hit all of her notes. When she was finished, she gave a quick bow and walked off stage.

"You did awesome!" Beyoncé's dad said. "Now let's see if it was enough to make the group."

"If we need to see you again, we will call you! If you don't receive a phone call, it means that the competition was really strong this year and, unfortunately, you were not chosen," a voice boomed out from the front of the auditorium. Beyoncé's dad squeezed her hand.

When they got home, Tina was waiting for them at their front door.

"They want you to be in the girl group! Five other girls made it as well!"

Beyoncé jumped up and down and Solange was cheering for her sister. Mathew and Tina looked at each other excitedly. A big star...

The first six girls in Girls Tyme were Beyoncé, Kelly Rowland (Beyoncé's cousin!), Ashley Támar Davis, Nina Taylor, Nikki Taylor and LaTavia Robinson. The girls were all around the same age and became fast friends as they spent a LOT of time together rehearsing. Nearly all of their time, come to think of it.

Of course, school had to come first. But after school they would go to the studio and perfect their moves. Then they would have singing lessons and put it all together into one big performance. And then they would practice... over and over and over again.

In 1992 the girls had a chance of a lifetime: to be on TV! The show was called *Star Search*, and it was a talent show that might give Girls Tyme the platform to sign a mega record deal.

The group performed well but they lost the show to their rivals, achieving three stars out of a possible four. After this Mathew Knowles, Beyoncé's dad, quit his job selling medical equipment to formally manage the group full-time.

Mathew cut the band down to four members, with Nina, Nikki and Ashley Támar out and LeToya Luckett in. The four girls maintained the same intense rehearsal schedule.

Aside from their brief appearance on *Star Search*, the group wasn't in the public eye. For a long time, no one knew who Girls Tyme was. They mostly performed at small venues or gatherings in Houston, Texas. This was not overnight stardom. It was a lot of hard work and not very much payoff.

Beyoncé knew working hard was the only way to succeed. So she kept learning, practicing, mastering. Learning, practicing, mastering.

There were many things Beyoncé had to wave goodbye to in exchange for working towards success. While other kids were playing sports for fun or going on dates or to the movies with their friends, Beyoncé was doing two things: school and

girl group practice. These were sacrifices, her dad would explain to her, but Beyoncé didn't need the explanation. She understood. She was giving up a lot in the hopes of getting a lot later down the road. She had a dream of being a big star.

By 1996 the band had a new name: Destiny's Child. With Beyoncé centered as the frontwoman, it started to make major waves in the music industry. Mathew had been running the band like a tight ship; a boot camp. But his boot camp... well, it had been working.

"We did choreography and vocal lessons and team building and we jogged for physical fitness. That's what we did all day," Mathew had said of his rehearsals.

Soon, Kelly and Beyoncé were the only two original girls in the group and they welcomed Michelle Williams, just as some of that hard work was beginning to pay off.

When Columbia Records signed the girl group, doors that had been closed before started to open for them at alarming speed.

In November 1997 their first hit with Columbia, "No, No, No", dropped on the airwaves. Beyoncé had just turned 16 years old. The track reached number three on the Billboard Hot 100 chart and was remixed by a famous rapper, Wyclef Jean.

It felt like all of Beyoncé's dreams were coming true, finally. She had worked so hard, and had secretly grumbled to herself about that work not paying off. But it turns out she just needed to wait patiently and not give up. Her moment had arrived. These young women were a force, and the world was about to meet that force, head-on.

FIRST, THEY WERE BEING CONSIDERED FOR THE RADIO. THEN, THEIR SONGS WERE BEING CONSIDERED FOR MOVIE SOUNDTRACKS!

Chapter 3

Finding Fame...
With and Without Friends

• • • • • • • • • • • •

Soon, everyone in the country was learning Beyoncé's name. Destiny's Child debuted their first album in February of 1998, but it didn't do so well—despite the hit single "No, No, No Part 2" (with Wyclef Jean). A year later they came out with their second album. Their success hinged on that second album being bigger than the first. Would it happen? Beyoncé wanted this dream so badly.

Beyoncé and the girls crossed their fingers on the day that second album came out. Would the radio stations play their songs? Would people like them?

Beyoncé thought about the grueling hours of practice, practice, practice. She thought about her sore feet and sore throat after singing too much. She thought about a lot of the things she missed out on—spending time with her friends, going to football games, parties, dances, school. If the Destiny's Child album bombed... she couldn't even think about it. The butterflies. This was it. Would the radio play their songs?

Boy, did they play their songs. The second album was called "The Writing's On The Wall" and radio stations played song after song, and people were still calling in to request to hear them more.

"I wanna hear "Bills, Bills, Bills!" said a girl who called her favorite radio station.

"Can you guys play "Say My Name"?" a woman requested when she called in to her favorite station.

"Play "Jumpin, Jumpin!" a man said excitedly when he finally got through to his favorite DJ.

(Remember this was before streaming allowed anyone to get any song on their computer!)

The album "The Writing's On The Wall", really solidified the band's stardom. Everyone was paying attention to them!

AND THIS WENT ON ALL YEAR. THE ALBUM WAS SELLING SO MANY COPIES, IT WAS HARD FOR STORES TO KEEP THE CD IN STOCK!

It was even nominated for six Grammy awards—the most prestigious award of the music industry.

Destiny's Child songs were everywhere. In movies, on the radio, on television. The album eventually went on to sell...

15. MILLION. COPIES. WORLDWIDE!

Everywhere they went they were treated like huge stars. When they would go to see their favorite singers in concert, they would automatically be treated to backstage passes and tours.

They had come a long way from Girls Tyme and performing at small events in Houston, Texas. Beyoncé had come a long way from those shy days on the school playground. Mathew and Tina were so proud and so excited. Solange was inspired by her sister. Most importantly, Beyoncé felt accomplished. She was even starting to be behind the scenes on Destiny's Child, writing and producing songs for the group.

Her hard work and sacrifice had yielded amazing results. She no longer felt grumpy that she'd missed parties and football games and dances and sleepovers as a kid. This was worth it.

It seemed like nothing could ever get better. But of course, this was only the beginning.

Destiny's Child was wildly successful as the world headed into the new millennium. In May 2001 their next studio album was released: "Survivor".

The album debuted at number one in nine countries and also got the nominations of two Grammys. How could things get better?

Beyoncé's dad had some new ideas, though. He was very invested in Beyoncé's success beyond Destiny's Child. He had seen what happens to some of these girl and boy groups—they go in and out of style like fashion trends. How could Beyoncé outlast being a "trend"?

He had some big plans, but he wanted to make sure Beyoncé would be on-board. One day, when it was just the two of them, he asked her a very important question.

"WHAT WOULD YOU THINK ABOUT GOING SOLO?" HE ASKED.

Beyoncé wasn't sure. Would she fall out with her friends Kelly and Michelle? But what if she stayed with the group and Destiny's Child went out of style?

She had to think about this. On one hand, she really did want to go solo. It had always been her dream to be a big star. On the other hand, Beyoncé loved and respected Kelly and Michelle. Would they feel it was a betrayal to explore a career in singing and performing without them? And what if they too tried to go solo, and flopped? Could their friendship survive?

There were those butterflies again.

"I have to think about it, Dad," she said. He nodded his head. He knew it was Beyoncé's decision to make.

Beyoncé thought and thought and thought about it.

"Dad," she started slowly. "I decided I want to try to go solo. I think Kelly and Michelle will be supportive of me."

Mathew was proud of his daughter. He knew that was a hard decision to make. But he was also excited for her future.

That decision was great for all the girls. Mathew had also been asking Kelly and Michelle the same thing, and the solo careers for all three were launched. Michelle released a successful gospel album and Kelly featured on a hit single called "Dilemma" with the artist Nelly.

As for Beyoncé, many amazing opportunities were waiting, just around the corner.

"I FELT LIKE IT WAS TIME TO SET UP MY FUTURE, SO I SET A GOAL. MY GOAL WAS INDEPENDENCE."

—Beyoncé Knowles

Chapter 4

I Want To Be An Icon

· · · · · · · · · · ·

"I want to be an icon," Beyoncé told a glossy magazine in September 2008. She was 26 at the time, and really starting to come into her own. She was using her voice and making herself known—not just as an entertainer but as someone people should be keeping their eyes on. "I am over being a pop star," she added.

The last eight years had been huge for Beyoncé. She had gone from girl group member to national entertainment superstar. She was now going solo, and her choice proved to be the correct one for her career. Beyoncé had released two mega studio albums and was dropping hit after hit after hit. She'd performed at the Super Bowl, toured around the world and was elevated into the spotlight with some of the most famous people in the world. And as much as people loved Destiny's Child, they were clamoring for Beyoncé, Beyoncé, Beyoncé.

Some people would say that Beyoncé's declaration—"I want to be an icon"—was a big turning point in her glittering career.

They were not wrong.

After all, this was the first time she was saying these dreams out loud to someone other than her parents and closest confidants. Now that she had said it to the world she was certain that she was going to have to do whatever it would take to make that dream—"I want to be an icon"—a reality.

> **HER EVOLUTION FROM GIRL BAND FRONTWOMAN TO INTERNATIONAL SUPERSTAR WAS TRULY AMAZING, YES, BUT IT CAME AT A MAJOR COST.**

Long days of grueling practices put pressure on her body and her voice. Her image was constantly under scrutiny, as it is for most celebrities. She had to be in her best mental, physical and emotional shape at all times. If she was feeling sick or under the weather or even having a bad day, she couldn't pull out of performances or rehearsals.

Lots of people may have quit once it got really hard! But not Beyoncé. She kept working and working, harder and harder every single day.

Beyoncé wakes up around 6am to stretch and greet the day and maybe even do a little meditation.

Many days she heads to the gym to exercise, because she needs to be fit to dance and sing at the same time.

Some days she'll learn new choreography, rehearse and practice until it's perfect for the big stage.

Other days she'll be on press tours, doing interviews with magazines or TV shows. Sometimes she'll do both in one day!

Exhausting! But she always makes time in her schedule for what is most important to her: time for friends and family. It keeps her centered.

This social time keeps her happy, balanced and ready for whatever the day might throw at her.

One of the hardest parts about being a celebrity is the work involved to maintain it. But when Beyoncé was on stage or in front of the cameras, she was smiling and perfect and her work looked so effortless.

> BUT PEOPLE PAYING CLOSE ATTENTION KNEW THE TRUTH — BEYONCÉ WAS A SWAN; LOOKING PERFECT AND POISED ON TOP, BUT PEDDLING FAST AND FURIOUS UNDERNEATH THE WATER.

She was always moving in one direction or another. She believed that was what it would take to be the icon she dreamed of being.

Eyes on the prize, Beyoncé.

She had made it so far, and because of that, it might have been really easy for her to sit back and relax. She knew better than that. She knew if she stopped moving, even for a second, she might lose her rhythm. Well, not literally of course! But have you ever been running really fast, and the second you stop you realize just how tired you are? That was the feeling Beyoncé was trying her very best to avoid!

Her new husband, rapper and entertainer Jay-Z, believed in Beyoncé's dreams. He knew his wife's star was still rising and he supported her. He and Beyoncé shared a similar work ethic. That means that they viewed their work and goals in similar ways, and that they wanted a lot of the same things for themselves and for each other.

And above all else, they believed in one thing: practice.

Here is a big secret that the biggest stars in the world know and now you can know, too: the biggest misconception of reaching stardom? That you no longer need to practice. Not so! Practicing was more important than ever. Do you know Broadway stars practice every day? Athletes practice all of the time. Professional singers still take voice lessons and work with coaches. In fact, these people practice so much that there is little time for anything else. This was when the word "priority" returned to Beyoncé's daily vocabulary. Wanting to be an icon meant she had to do more than want it. She needed to live like an icon would. It was a life of glamor, yes, but also hard work and effort.

Maybe the most important quality Beyoncé had was that she truly, deeply loved all that was required of her to reach her dreams; even the bad days. Even the days when her voice and body needed a break. Loving the work was how she knew in her heart and in her soul that she would one day be known as an icon.

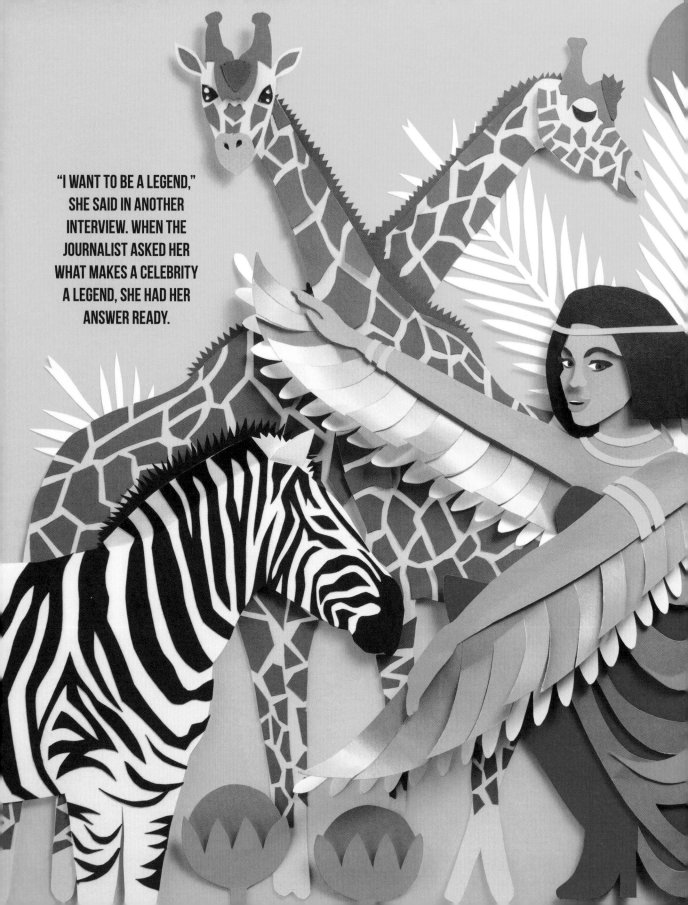

"I WANT TO BE A LEGEND," SHE SAID IN ANOTHER INTERVIEW. WHEN THE JOURNALIST ASKED HER WHAT MAKES A CELEBRITY A LEGEND, SHE HAD HER ANSWER READY.

"WHEN YOU SAY HER NAME, WHAT YOU THINK ABOUT IS HER STAR QUALITY. SHE IS A GOOD PERSON, HAS GOOD SPIRIT, AND IS MORE THAN JUST A PERSON WHO PERFORMS AND SELLS RECORDS. SHE'S A PERSON WHO WILL CHANGE YOUR LIFE."

—Beyoncé Knowles

Chapter 5

Empowered To Be Fierce... Sasha Fierce

. . . .

As Beyoncé pumped out songs like "Irreplaceable" and "Ring the Alarm", the world was starting to get a sense of what she believed and what she valued. Through music, Beyoncé was putting out messages of female empowerment, feminism, and independence.

While some people spoke their beliefs and others wrote their beliefs, Beyoncé let hers shine through her songs.

Beyoncé had to make some big choices throughout her career. One of the biggest was figuring out what image she wanted to portray to the world. The press and fans were hungry for Beyoncé, and while that was flattering, it could be overwhelming! Beyoncé wanted to be an artist, a musician, an icon (as she said before!). She didn't necessarily want to share her entire life with everyone. Some things, she decided, were meant to be private. Like her family life. She wanted to keep her internal family goings-on out of the public eye.

But she had to give the public something to keep them interested in her, without giving too much of herself.

SUDDENLY, SHE HAD AN IDEA. AN ALTER-EGO!

Just like Clark Kent would change into Superman, just like Miley Cyrus moonlighted as Hannah Montana, Beyoncé would come up with an alter-ego.

Her alter-ego would need a great name. Beyoncé thought and thought and thought about it.

What about... Sasha Fierce?

Sasha Fierce would be Beyoncé's onstage persona. She would be the personality and the attitude she'd push onto the rest of the world, so that she could be free to be Beyoncé in her private time. Beyoncé used Sasha Fierce as a persona who could experiment with new things. She even came up with an two-disc album called "I am Sasha Fierce". The first disc, "I am", featured slower and mid-tempo songs that came from the heart. The second, "Sasha Fierce", was filled with dance and rap-inspired hits that were presented by Sasha – not Beyoncé.

Sasha is unapologetic, confident, loud, outspoken, honest and unique.

One of her biggest hits came out of "I am Sasha Fierce". That year, 2008, was the year the song "Single Ladies" was released. Do you know it?

You might! Ask an adult if they know it. I bet they do.

In 2008 and 2009 "Single Ladies" seemed to be on every radio station all day long. The music video was everywhere, and everyone was doing the "Single Ladies" dance. In the video, Beyoncé used all of those dancing skills she honed as a kid to perform an absolutely smashing piece of choreography. People were learning the dances in their own living rooms and bedrooms—like Beyoncé had done with her favorite songs as a kid—and performing their own Single Ladies dances for their friends. Parties and weddings weren't complete without a bunch of revelers performing the "Single Ladies" dance— even if they weren't as good at dancing as Beyoncé was!

Beyoncé was ubiquitous. That word means that she was everywhere, all the time. Everyone knew her name. It felt like there were a lot of risks; like there were a lot of eyes on her and she wanted to be absolutely perfect. Beyoncé started to get very involved in the business elements of her career. While her father was her manager, Beyoncé wanted him to be very transparent in all of his decision making so that she could give some of her input. This is where Beyoncé truly shined. She loved to have a big hand in her own success. She never sent "Sasha" to the business meetings. This was something she knew she didn't need an alter-ego for.

But Beyoncé and her dad started butting heads. That can happen!

LEARN THE MOVES TO 'SINGLE LADIES'

They were both adults and they were both passionate about Beyoncé's career. Her dad had been making lots of good deals for Beyoncé—she signed a big commercial deal with a major soda brand and she was getting invites to perform at major events. She had already been in a few movies and was trying to figure out if she wanted to keep up with acting. She was getting lots of offers to do lots of different things... but all of those offers were floating around her head and making her feel a little dizzy.

That's when Parkwood Entertainment was born. Beyoncé wasn't just about singing and dancing. She was about the business. She wanted control of every aspect of her brand. Beyoncé no longer needed her dad professionally. "I started my own company when I decided to manage myself. It was important that I didn't go to some big management company, I felt like I wanted to ... be a powerhouse and have my own empire, and show other women when you get to this point in your career you don't have to go sign with someone else and share your money and your success – you do it yourself."

By 2010, it had been ten whole years since Beyoncé had started her solo career. She had starred in movies, put out dozens of hit songs and half a dozen hit albums. She had set her eyes on new sights and new heights, she had gotten married,

she had experienced pain and joy.

And she—just like a runner who finally slows down—was exhausted.

> # BEYONCÉ WAS STARTING TO FEEL A LITTLE TIRED. ACTUALLY, SHE WAS STARTING TO FEEL A LOT TIRED.

It would be hard to take a break. Remember, her entire career had been built on not taking a break! Beyoncé had learned to see taking a break as being sort of weak. We know that isn't true (everyone needs some down time once in a while), but Beyoncé was ever the perfectionist and she didn't allow herself such luxuries. Deep down she worried that it might mean she was a failure or that she couldn't "hack it" as a star. She was a people pleaser and she feared her fans would start thinking she was lazy.

But her whole message was that of empowerment. Of being unapologetic! Of asking for what you need. Beyoncé realized she needed to practice what she preached. She needed to be empowered! She needed to be unapologetic. She needed to ask for what she needed.

She needed this break.

This was what people meant by "a new chapter" and Beyoncé was about to turn the page and start hers.

BEYONCÉ

DANCE!

WHAT OPRAH SAID!

BREATHE

Run the World

GIRLS
GIRLS
GIRLS
GIRLS
GIRLS

FEMALE POWER

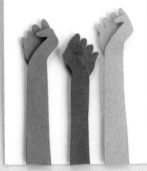

TAKE
a
BREAK

BEYONCÉ

Chapter 6

Life Is But A Dream

• • • • • • • • • • • •

During her hiatus from music, Beyoncé and Jay-Z thought it might be time to fulfill a secret dream they had kept to themselves. They wanted to be parents. They wanted to have a baby.

It wouldn't be so easy. Beyoncé encountered difficulties and heartbreak trying to start a family.

"THIS IS THE SADDEST THING I HAVE EVER ENDURED," BEYONCÉ WOULD LATER SAY OF THIS TIME IN HER LIFE.

Up until that point, throughout the hiatus, Beyoncé had not felt the urge to return to music. But she could only think of one true way for her heart to heal—to write songs about it. Beyoncé got back into the studio and wrote many of the songs that would soon appear on her album, "4".

When Beyoncé and Jay-Z were in Paris to finalize the album art for "4", they found out they were pregnant.

"4" was the first album to come out after Beyoncé's break from music, and

fans were going crazy for it. The album had hit song after hit song after hit song. Beyoncé performed "4" at the famous Glastonbury music festival in the UK— the first female soloist to headline the main stage in two decades. What a way to make herstory!

When it came to these performances from her new album, there was one track that was taking over the world.

It was "Love On Top", a happy and boppy pop number that featured the singer changing keys several times throughout the song to show off her range. If you thought that "Single Ladies" was a success, then it had some competition with "Love On Top".

When MTV asked her to perform "Love On Top" at the 2011 Video Music Awards, Beyoncé decided this would be a great time to tell the world her good news. We know that Beyoncé liked to reveal intimate details of her life through her work, so you can probably guess how she announced her pregnancy...

Yep! That's right. Beyoncé performed "Love On Top" at the VMAs and ended the song by opening her jacket to reveal her pregnant belly. It was a wild

moment. No one knew! People went crazy. Jay-Z was in the audience as his friends surrounded him, cheering and applauding.

Beyoncé was officially the queen of the surprise! Her pregnancy announcement quickly became the most-watched VMA broadcast with over 12 million viewers. Wow! It became one of the most talked about pop culture moments in recent history. She was making headlines! Things were looking way up for Beyoncé. All she needed to do was take some time to herself to reset, and she was able to come back better than ever. She even sang at one of the biggest events in American history: President Obama's second term inauguration! In fact, she and the President and Michelle Obama had become friends.

WAS THIS REAL LIFE? SHE'D WONDER. PINCH ME; I AM DREAMING!

She was so happy she had gone ahead with that big break. That break from music had helped open her up to new experiences.

Now she was ready to sing again... and she had so many wonderful things to sing about.

Parkwood Entertainment began to take off in a big way. While Beyoncé kept the most intimate parts of her pregnancy private, she was still working behind the scenes at Parkwood to keep everything in motion. Working at Parkwood Entertainment was a really big deal, and employees were supposed to keep everything that was happening in the office a secret.

In fact, it wasn't too out of the ordinary for an employee at Parkwood to be in the dark about certain projects. Parkwood employees would ask each other, 'Do you have any idea?' They usually wouldn't!

Behind the scenes of Beyoncé's pregnancy, something big was cooking at Parkwood... Beyoncé was making a full-length documentary of her life while pregnant called "Life Is But A Dream" which was released on HBO. This movie married so many parts of Beyoncé's business sense. She would let fans into the intimate parts of her life... but her only rule was that she was in charge of producing every second that they would see. She was a fabulous performer and so very talented, yes, but she had real business genius.

Beyoncé was starting to realize her passion and dream of becoming an icon wouldn't just happen by performing. It would happen by being a well-rounded businesswoman.

It wouldn't be easy, but she was ready for the task.

Chapter 7
The Biggest Secret...
Revealed

· · · · · · · · · · · ·

Ever since dropping "Life Is But A Dream" Beyoncé became addicted to the element of surprise. She vowed to incorporate surprises as often as she could.

If you weren't sure by now, Jay-Z and Beyoncé were arguably two of the most well-known and famous people in the world, with a net worth of millions between them. This allowed them opportunities most people do not get, especially not those who have just given birth to babies.

> BEING A MOM, ESPECIALLY BEING A MOM TO A LITTLE GIRL, MADE BEYONCÉ EVEN MORE AWARE OF HER DUTIES AS A WOMAN.

She realized she wanted to use her music and her art to empower women, especially Black women; to teach them that they could stand on their own and be strong. Looking at little Blue Ivy, she found all of the inspiration she would ever need. But she also looked to strong women for inspiration, saying that both Oprah and Michelle Obama were inspiring to her.

"My daughter introduced me to myself," she said in an exclusive interview with Oprah. "You know, my mother and I are so close, and I always prayed that I would have that type of relationship with my daughter. And she's still a baby, but the connection I had with her when I was giving birth was something that I've never felt before."

It was this inspiration that pushed Beyoncé through the work she felt she had to do after giving birth. It was this inspiration that helped solidify her purpose, not just as a pop star or even as an icon, but as an influential entertainment legend, who used her art to spread powerful messages no one would ever be able to ignore, even long after she had left this world.

Beyoncé worked, and worked, and worked on this secret project. Those who were employed to work on this project with her were sworn to secrecy. Luckily,

she had a really trustworthy team of people who really liked working with and for her. They just knew that part of Beyoncé's appeal was the fact that so much of her work was done out of the public eye until it was ready to go on display. It was part of the art itself.

Beyoncé worked, and she worked hard. Of course, no one outside #TeamBeyoncé knew that. They just assumed she was laying low to be with Jay-Z and the new baby girl Blue Ivy. Partially that was true.

But the other part that no one knew was that Beyoncé was hard at work on her biggest album yet.

This would be the first album to drop after Beyoncé became a mother. It was a celebration of the love she had for her family and the love she had for herself as an empowered Black woman and artist. She wanted her art to shout her values from the rooftops, and because of that, every song had to be perfect.

Finally, it was time.

December 13, 2013, the clock struck midnight, and quietly, Beyoncé dropped her new album on iTunes without telling anyone beforehand.

PEOPLE. WENT. NUTS.

"Um," said someone on Twitter. "A new Beyoncé album is up on iTunes!"

"Whoa," tweeted someone else. "NEW BEYONCÉ!"

In less than an hour, the album had been downloaded nearly 100,000 times. People were texting and calling their friends who were asleep, telling them to go online that second to hear the new album.

Beyoncé's big plan had worked. She had managed to shock the world by dropping her fifth studio album without anyone knowing it was happening.

Iconic. That was the word people were using to describe the superstar's ability to capture the entire entertainment world without leveraging any sort of press or marketing. It was truly special.

The album—called "Beyoncé"— was Beyoncé's fifth number one album in America, making her the first woman in Billboard's chart history to achieve this status. By the end of the week, the album sold over one million digital copies worldwide and delivered hit after hit after hit, including collaborative songs with Jay-Z and a song "Flawless" that featured powerful feminist prose from author Chimamanda Ngozi Adichie's "We should all be feminists".

Beyoncé was no longer just the pop star she was in the mid-2000s. 2010s Beyoncé was proving herself to be legendary. Just as she always knew she would be.

BEYONCÉ

Nº. 1

"I KNOW I'M STRONGER IN
THE SONGS THAN I REALLY AM.
SOMETIMES I NEED TO HEAR
IT MYSELF. WE ALL NEED
TO HEAR THOSE EMPOWERING
SONGS TO REMIND US."

—Beyoncé Knowles

Chapter 8

People Are Listening

· · · · · · · · · · ·

Soon after the secret Beyoncé album dropped, the star declared herself to be a feminist in British Vogue.

> ### SHE SAID: "I AM A MODERN-DAY FEMINIST. I DO BELIEVE IN EQUALITY."

What does being a feminist mean? Well, that's actually a very easy question to answer.

This is the definition of feminist: believing that men and women are equal.

After Blue Ivy was born, Beyoncé realized just how important it was going to be to make her life's work about the empowerment of her fellow woman. That's why "Flawless", was such a major part of her surprise album. Beyoncé recognised the power in Chimamanda Ngozi Adichie's words: "We say to girls, 'You can have ambition, but not too much.'" She used the words to bring the world's attention to feminist issues.

Beyoncé realized her music could be an even bigger vehicle for change. People were listening.

She had to sit down and really think about the things she cared about. The things that meant a lot to her. The things that defined her not just as an artist, but as a human being. As a member of her community. As a member of the world.

Over the next few years, her opinions and morals would be challenged, and she'd be using her voice to do much more than sing songs.

Soon she would have her chance to stop people in their tracks.

"32-year-old Philando Castile was shot to death tonight by a Minnesota

police officer after being pulled over," Beyoncé heard a news anchor say in 2016. "Castile was driving with his girlfriend and young daughter when he was pulled over in a routine traffic stop."

A routine traffic stop is when a police officer can pull over a car for any reason, and has

VOGUE

"I AM A
MODERN-DAY
FEMINIST. "

the power to search it. The problem was, Black people were pulled over in these routine stops in greater numbers than everyone else. And it was particularly worrying because they were also more likely to experience violence in these scary situations.

Beyoncé felt sick to her stomach. She knew that Black men and women were suffering, leading to a cry from the Black community and their allies in America: Black Lives Matter.

BLACK LIVES MATTER MEANS "BLACK LIVES MATTER AS MUCH AS ANY LIFE DOES" AND NOT "BLACK LIVES MATTER MORE THAN OTHER LIVES".

That's the most important thing to understand about the movement.

Beyoncé knew she could not sit back and look at the injustice being perpetrated against her own community. It was time to use her voice—not just her art—to influence the world around her.

Beyoncé called her manager and asked for a statement to be added to her website ahead of a tour performance that week.

"I am frustrated and angry and upset," Beyoncé said. "This statement reflects that."

Soon her website would read:

www.beyonce.com

"THESE ROBBERIES OF LIVES MAKE US FEEL HELPLESS AND HOPELESS BUT WE HAVE TO BELIEVE THAT WE ARE FIGHTING FOR THE RIGHTS OF THE NEXT GENERATION, FOR THE NEXT YOUNG MEN AND WOMEN WHO BELIEVE IN GOOD."

A few nights later she sang her political song, "Freedom", without background musicians, in front of the names of Black men, women and children who had been murdered by police. Beyoncé called for a moment of silence for Philando Castile "and countless others."

It was very powerful, and Beyoncé felt that power.

Later that week, her husband made his own statement, *The New York Times* reported, releasing a song "motivated by anger—and exhaustion—about police brutality, in which Jay-Z repeats the refrain "Just a boy from the 'hood that/Got my hands in the air/In despair, don't shoot.""

Beyoncé and Jay-Z had officially taken their stance as a couple against the injustices of being Black in America. It would soon be revered as a very important stance to take.

Chapter 9

Respect. Our. Lives.

· · · · · · · · · · · ·

Her fans were clamoring for more. This was the Beyoncé they loved. Not just the incredible artist but the social activist, too. A group of her most ardent supporters labeled themselves the BeyHive (pronounced beehive!). Beyoncé, who once kept her personal opinions and intimate thoughts to herself, was starting to see the benefit in sharing her true beliefs with the world.

"She'd made a decision to live a more authentic life, and since that time, she'd endeavored to do just that. She'd quietly gone about the business of separating the parts of her life that felt true and organic from those that felt false and pretentious, and then moved forward committed to personal honesty and integrity."

But not everyone was happy about this decision.

Some people accused Beyoncé of being too rich and out of touch with the masses to truly care about what was happening in the world around her. It was true; she was one of the richest women in the entertainment industry, and along with her husband, they were extremely powerful. But that did not mean she could not care about Black Lives Matter.

Others criticized the couple for not "staying in their lane"—they wanted Jay-Z and Beyoncé to "shut up and sing". That was something Beyoncé had worried about in the past. She cared what people thought about her, but she realized as she grew up that she cared way more about what she thought of herself.

> ## IF PEOPLE WANTED TO JUDGE HER FOR BEING ON THE RIGHT SIDE OF HISTORY, THAT WOULD BE THEIR DECISION TO MAKE.

In the meantime, the BeyHive and her other loyal fans were drowning out the sounds of the naysayers. There were way more fans and supporters than there were detractors. This is super important when you're on your way to success. When Beyoncé would announce a performance, the tickets would sell out nearly immediately. Everyone wanted to just be in the same room as the one and only Beyoncé.

There will always be people looking down on you but you have to look for the people who are propping you up and

SORRY
NOT SORRY
BLACK LIVES MATTER
BOSS
UNSTOPPABLE
GRL PWR
Feminist

believing in you. And most of all, you have to believe in yourself!

> ### IF HER ALBUM, "4" WAS ABOUT LOVE AND HER SURPRISE ALBUM WAS ABOUT FEMINISM AND SELF-LOVE... THEN HER 2016 RELEASE, "LEMONADE", WAS ABOUT ABSOLUTE EMPOWERMENT.

Beyoncé sang songs about her own life in "Lemonade"—and not just the good parts. There are sad songs, too. And angry songs. And joyful songs, and songs about learning lessons. But there were also really cool elements of "Lemonade" that would make it legendary. For one, it was a visual album. "Lemonade" was released with an hour-long film accompanying it on TV—and millions of people tuned in to watch. That was Beyoncé—she could always captivate a crowd!

She also chose this album to collaborate with musicians and talent far and wide—nearly one hundred of them! Beyoncé knew that working alone would leave her in ultimate control, but she also knew that working with other talent would allow her to grow exponentially (that means by a lot!).

That meant everyone involved in the project had to keep this very big secret (just like last time, and all of the time!). Beyoncé had commanded a level of respect that meant she could ask people to keep this very big secret.

Singer-songwriter Jonny Coffer said of Beyoncé and "Lemonade": "She runs the show and will say what she likes and doesn't like and is always making suggestions. She knows exactly how she wants it to sound and how to get there."

The album had a number of anthems on it, the biggest of which might be the song "Formation" which was a battle cry for women everywhere. It was also the song that kicked off Beyoncé's biggest world tour to date— the FORMATION world tour, and had already been introduced to audiences at the Super Bowl earlier that year.

The album "Lemonade" also paved the way for her next visual album: "Black is King". This high-production masterpiece is a celebration of Blackness across Africa, America and the world. It is no wonder that Beyoncé called it her "passion project". Blue Ivy even made several cameos and sang in the song "Brown Skin Girl". Like mother, like daughter!

"NEVER LET SUCCESS GO TO YOUR HEAD.

NEVER LET FAILURE GET TO YOUR HEART."

—Beyoncé Knowles

Chapter 10

Find Your Inner Beyoncé

· · · · · · · · · · ·

Beyoncé has done so much to achieve her legendary icon status. Hit songs? Check. "Single Ladies", "Formation", "Crazy in Love"... the list goes on and on!

Starring in movies? The Lion King, DreamGirls, Austin Powers... check.

Winning dozens of huge awards? 23 Grammys, 28 MTV VMAs, Critics' Choice Award... check.

Donating her voice (and money, and time) to the important causes she believes in? Check.

But she has perhaps done one thing that is more important than all of these combined. Now I know what you're thinking! You're thinking, *huh? What are you talking about? What else could there possibly be?*

BEYONCÉ HAS EMPOWERED A GENERATION OF WOMEN AND MEN —MULTIPLE GENERATIONS, IN FACT —TO BELIEVE IN THEMSELVES AND THE POWER THAT THEY HAVE INSIDE TO CREATE CHANGE IN THE WORLD AROUND THEM.

Beyoncé, by rising to the top through hard work, has shown little girls and boys that they too can reach for their dreams and make them true..

Beyoncé is a hero to so many people who look up to her, and her music is a source of strength to her fans.

But we know she didn't get there by taking an easy road. We know that she made sacrifices and took risks. We know that while other children were going to school dances and after school playdates, Beyoncé was focusing on her long-term dreams and goals. There's nothing wrong or bad about going to school dances and having play dates with friends, but Beyoncé showed us from an early age that if you're serious about your dreams, you can start working towards them at any time!

She knew all dreams start with being true to yourself and she wanted to empower a new generation to believe that too. And it all started by listening to that voice inside her.

If she listened to her own voice, then others would listen to their own voices. And she did. And they did.

START

"IT'S EASY TO HEAR THE VOICES OF OTHERS AND OFTEN VERY DIFFICULT TO HEAR YOUR OWN.

EVERY PERSON YOU MEET IS GOING TO WANT SOMETHING DIFFERENT FROM YOU.

THE QUESTION IS:
"WHAT DO YOU WANT FOR YOURSELF?"

—Beyoncé Knowles

Rule the music scene like Beyoncé!

10 key lessons from Beyoncé Knowles's life

1 **It's okay to be shy! But don't let it keep you from trying new things.** Beyoncé was a shy girl, which is a wonderful characteristic. Are you shy too? That is special. I bet it seems like some people who aren't shy have no problem trying new things. Trying new things can be scary for everyone, whether you are shy or outgoing. It's important to believe in your ability to try new things just like Beyoncé tried taking a dance class!

2 **Successful people know that working hard everyday is the key to achieving their goals.** Beyoncé was not an overnight sensation. If it were possible to be an overnight sensation, we all would be superstars! Keep working hard.

3 **Your definition of success might look different from someone else's.** We are all capable of being the best and most successful versions of ourselves and only we can decide what that means!

4 **You don't have to feel "in love" with your dreams every minute of the day.** Sometimes you may want to take a break from your hard work and try something new. You may think this means you don't believe in your dreams. Don't listen to that voice in your head. Everyone needs to take a break sometimes! It is healthy and smart to honor that!

5 **Find your voice.** Beyoncé is a singer and a performer, of course, but she does more with her voice than singing. She uses her voice to give power to those who do not have it. She uses her voice to draw attention to the issues she cares about. We all have an important voice... how will you use yours?

6 **Sometimes you're at the top, and sometimes you're on the bottom: Embrace both!**
If you have ever had a really terrible day followed by a really great day, you know what it's like to experience vastly different emotions in a short period of time. Sometimes you will achieve dreams and it will feel better than you could have ever imagined. Sometimes you will fail and it will feel bad and discouraging. You can learn from these experiences!

7 **It is okay to keep things private.**
You are entitled to privacy. Many people think that because big stars like Beyoncé are in the public eye that their lives are open books for everyone to read. No matter how famous you are or aren't, everyone is allowed to have boundaries and privacy. Respect the privacy of others and make sure you ask people to respect yours as well.

8 **The only person who needs to believe in you is you!**
I bet you have more than one person who believes in you, so you're already ahead of the game.

9 **Giving back is important.**
Beyoncé has used her fame and fortune to support causes and movements she believes in. You can do that too.

10 **If you know who you are on the inside, no one can change who you are on the outside.**
Beyonce is true to herself, no matter what anyone else says. It is important that you are true to yourself, too.

Grab a sheet of paper & a pencil and answer these questions!

Beyoncé found fame young with Destiny's Child.
If the same thing happened to you, who would be in your band?
What would your band be called?
What songs would you sing?

. . . .

Imagine you were a pop star like Beyoncé.
What would be your daily routine?
How hard would you work?

. . . .

If you were famous, how would you deal with your privacy?
Would you feel comfortable sharing your life with the world or
would you shut it out?

. . . .

Beyoncé supports the movements that are important to her.
What would make you take a stand?
How would you make a difference?

Further Reading

· · · · · · · · · · · ·

Take a look at these other great books and resources to learn more about Beyoncé. You can also read about and help the organizations she supports, or has founded, listed below.

Non-fiction

Queen Bey: A Celebration of the Power and Creativity of Beyoncé Knowles-Carter by Veronica Chambers
Beyoncégraphica: A Graphic Biography of Beyoncé by Chris Roberts
Young, Gifted and Black by Jamia Wilson and Andrea Pippins

Advanced Reading

Becoming Beyoncé: The Untold Story by J. Randy Taraborrelli
Beyoncé: Running the World: The Biography by Anna Pointer
Beyoncé in Formation: Remixing Black Feminism by Omise'eke Natasha Tinsley
JAY-Z: Made in America by Michael Eric Dyson
We Should All Be Feminists by Chimamanda Ngozi Adichie

Organizations

BeyGood
Survivor Foundation
CHIME FOR CHANGE
Feeding America
The Houston Food Bank

To my family, who has always taken my dreams seriously.—C.M.
To Lucia and Willow who should keep on dancing.—S.E.

Brimming with creative inspiration, how-to projects, and useful information to enrich your everyday life, Quarto Knows is a favourite destination for those pursuing their interests and passions. Visit our site and dig deeper with our books into your area of interest: Quarto Creates, Quarto Cooks, Quarto Homes, Quarto Lives, Quarto Drives, Quarto Explores, Quarto Gifts, or Quarto Kids.

First published in 2021 by Frances Lincoln Children's Books, an imprint of The Quarto Group. 400 First Avenue North, Suite 400, Minneapolis, MN 55401, USA.T (612) 344-8100 F (612) 344-8692 **www.QuartoKnows.com**

ISBN 978-0-7112-4947-9

The illustrations were created in paper

Set in Brandon Grotesque and Bebas Neue

Published by Katie Cotton

Designed by Sinem Erkas

Paper Modelling by Sinem Erkas and Christopher Noulton

Paper Assistants: Tijen Erkas, Nick Gentry, Lora Hristova

Edited by Katy Flint and Hattie Grylls

Production by Dawn Cameron

Manufactured in Guangdong, China TT052021

9 8 7 6 5 4 3 2 1

Photographic acknowledgements: p14, Destiny's Child poses on a couch in Beyoncé's house May 20, 2000 in Houston, TX. © Pam Francis/ Liaison via Getty Images; p32, Singer Beyoncé Knowles on stage at the 50th Annual GRAMMY Awards at the Staples Center on February 10, 2008 in Los Angeles, California © Michael Caulfield/WireImage via Getty Images; p46, Jay Z, Beyoncé and Blue Ivy Carter onstage at the 2014 MTV Video Music Awards at The Forum on August 24, 2014 in Inglewood, California © Jason LaVeris/FilmMagic via Getty Images.